3|95

BODIES IN CRISIS

COMMUNICABLE DISEASES

Jacqueline L. Harris

Twenty-First Century Books

A Division of Henry Holt and Company
New York

Twenty-First Century Books
A Division of Henry Holt and Company, Inc.
115 West 18th Street
New York, New York 10011

Henry Holt® and colophon are registered trademarks of Henry Holt and Company, Inc.
Publishers since 1866

Published in Canada by Fitzhenry & Whiteside Ltd.
195 Allstate Parkway, Markham, Ontario L3R 4T8

Printed in Mexico
All first editions are printed on acid-free paper.

Created and produced in association with Blackbirch Graphics, Inc.

Library of Congress Cataloging-in-Publication Data

Harris, Jacqueline L.
    Communicable diseases / Jacqueline L. Harris. — 1st. ed.
        p.   cm. — (Bodies in crisis)
    Includes bibliographical references and index.
    Summary: Explains communicable diseases, the body's physical reactions to them, and methods of prevention and treatment.
    ISBN 0-8050-2599-5 (acid-free paper)
    1. Communicable diseases—Juvenile literature. [1. Communicable diseases.]
    I. Title. II. Series.
    RC111.H37 1993
    616.9—dc20   93-25850
                                                                                    CIP
                                                                                    AC

Contents

Many communicable diseases make a person feel tired and achy. Fever, chills, and lack of appetite are some other common symptoms.

Getting Sick

A communicable disease is one that can be passed from one person or animal to another. Most communicable diseases are caused by small life-forms. Jeremy, Sean, Julie, and Carlos have all had experiences with different communicable diseases.

After a date one night, Jeremy walked Kelly home. On the doorstep, after making plans for another date, Jeremy leaned over and kissed Kelly good night. Several days later, as he was getting dressed for school, Jeremy suddenly felt chilly. He began to feel tired, and his throat was scratchy and sore. His mother took his temperature and ordered him back to bed. Then she made an appointment with Jeremy's doctor.

At the office, the doctor looked down Jeremy's throat. It was red, and there were white patches in the back. Jeremy had strep throat. A bacterium, one of those small life-forms we just talked about, had done this to Jeremy. The bacterium had passed from Kelly to him when they kissed each other. Small lumps on the sides of Jeremy's neck were signs that his body was working to get rid of the bacterial infection. The doctor gave Jeremy medicine to help his body fight the infection. After a few days, Jeremy felt much better.

Sean felt as though he were getting the flu as he dragged himself up to bed for the night. He felt tired and feverish. The next morning, he awoke with a head-ache, but he went off to his tenth-grade classes anyway. For the next few weeks, Sean struggled with a mildly sick feeling. Then it went away.

About a year later, Sean noticed some lumps in his groin, under his arms, and in his neck. He felt fine, but the lumps didn't go away. Several years later, Sean noticed white spots and sores in his mouth and on his tongue. A week later, sores appeared around his mouth and on his lower body around his anus. Fuzzy white patches had developed on his tongue. Then came diarrhea and a sudden and rapid weight loss. He began having trouble breathing, which signaled the onset of pneumonia, an infection of the lungs.

At the hospital, the doctor examining Sean had bad news. Sean had AIDS, a disease that is often transmitted sexually. Sean had disregarded lectures in high school that advised using condoms during sex.

A few months later, Sean's weight went down to 85 pounds, and he lost his sight. It was not long before he died. A virus had done this to Sean. It had robbed his

HOW HIV (THE AIDS VIRUS) AFFECTS THE IMMUNE SYSTEM

Normal Immune System

A person with a healthy immune system has various types of lymphocytes that combat any invading disease organisms.

Immune System in an AIDS Victim

A person with the HIV virus has a weakened immune system. In some cases, this weakness may lead to the series of infections known as AIDS.

Disease organisms   **T4–lymphocytes**

HIV   **T4–lymphocytes**

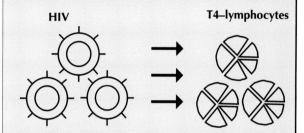

1 T4– lymphocytes and other immune system components in the body are alerted when they detect disease organisms.

1 HIV (the AIDS virus) actually multiplies within the body's T4 – lymphocytes and may ultimately destroy them.

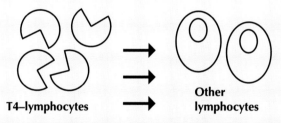

T4–lymphocytes

Other lymphocytes

Destroyed T4–lymphocytes

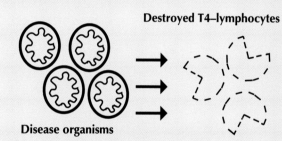

Disease organisms

2 In response to the invading organisms, the T4–lymphocytes help to regulate the response of other lymphocytes (cells of the immune system)

2 When the disease organisms invade other areas of the body, the immune responses may fail, due to absence of the vital T4-lymphocytes.

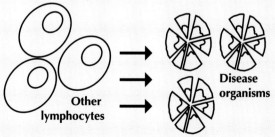

Other lymphocytes

Disease organisms

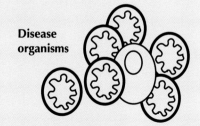

Disease organisms

3 The alerted lymphocytes then attack and destroy the disease organisms in various ways.

3 The disease organisms may overwhelm the immune system and lead to a series of infections commonly known as AIDS.

body of its ability to fight infection. The virus had been passed on to him by a high school classmate during sexual intercourse.

Basketball practice was over, and everyone was showering and racing around the locker room, getting changed. Julie dried herself quickly, dressed, and sat down on a bench near the shower room in order to put on her socks and shoes. The floor was wet, and Julie pulled her socks on right over her wet feet.

About 10 days later, Julie developed an itch between her toes. The skin between her toes began to crack and peel, and thin, clear fluid came out of the cracks. Constant soreness and itching continued for three months. Julie had athlete's foot. A fungus had done this to Julie. It was passed on to her on the wet floor by one of her teammates.

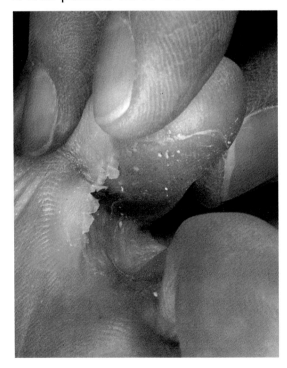

Athlete's foot is an infection of the skin between the toes that is caused by a fungus. Wet or damp areas that are cool provide ideal breeding grounds for the fungus.

Before Carlos came to the United States, he used to help his father cut sugarcane in Costa Rica. One day, in Costa Rica, a mosquito landed on his arm. Carlos swatted the mosquito as it bit into his flesh. The next week, Carlos developed a severe headache

Reported Cases of Common Communicable Diseases, 1991

Gonorrhea	602,600	Encephalitis	999
Syphilis	41,000	Typhus fever, tick-borne	635
AIDS	35,488	Typhoid fever	456
Tuberculosis	23,500	Toxic shock syndrome	274
Aseptic meningitis	14,102	Tularemia	188
Rabies, in animals	6,486	Leprosy (Hansen's disease)	140
Mumps	4,000	Brucellosis (undulant fever)	89
Pertussis (whooping cough)	2,600	Trichinosis	61
Meningococcal infections	1,998	Tetanus	49
Rubella (German measles)	1,400	Plague	10
Legionnellosis	1,222	Diphtheria	2
Malaria	1,173	Poliomyelitis	0

and became sick to his stomach. He hurt all over. His father made him stay home and rest.

A few days later, while lying on his bed, watching a soccer match on television, Carlos began to shiver. Then his temperature started to soar, and the pain in his head and back caused him to toss and turn. Next, Carlos began to perspire, drenching his clothes and the bed. After several hours, an exhausted Carlos fell asleep. When he awoke, he felt better, but two days later, his symptoms returned. If the doctor hadn't given Carlos medicine, Carlos would have continued to have attacks of chills and fever for two months or longer.

Carlos had malaria. A tiny, one-celled parasite had invaded Carlos's blood cells and made him sick. The organism was indirectly transferred to his body from another malaria victim through the bite of a certain mosquito. This mosquito is commonly found in tropical countries like the one in which Carlos had lived.

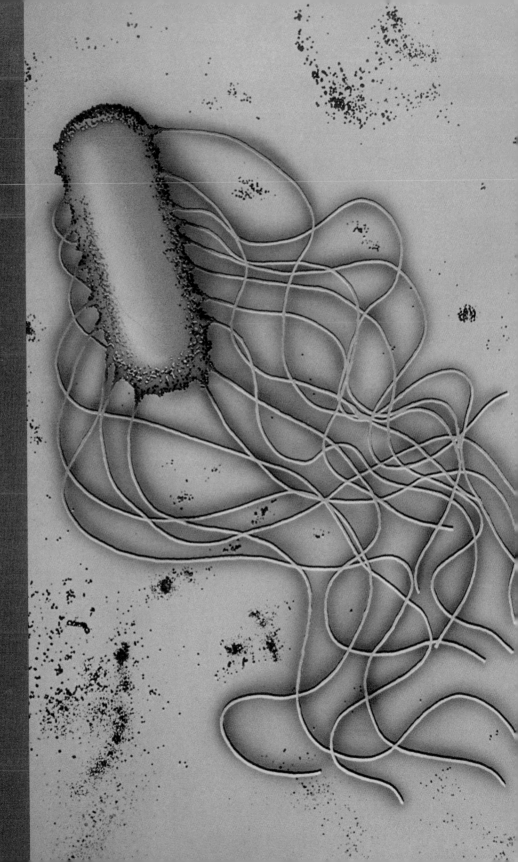

This enlarged photograph shows a single salmonella bacterium inside a human body. Salmonella, which causes a kind of food poisoning, is often present in eggs and poultry and will become harmless only if the food is thoroughly cooked.

2

Invasion of the Body

How do tiny organisms, most of which you can see only through the lens of a microscope, cause so much trouble?

Our world is full of tiny organisms. Some are good for our health, but others can make us sick. There are organisms in humans and animals that can be passed from person to person through air, water, and food.

Organisms can also be passed on through direct contact, as through an animal bite or sexual relations.

The human body is like a fortress. It is designed to prevent organisms from entering it. Two layers of skin cover the entire body. Eyebrows and eyelashes protect the eyes, and tiny hairs filter air going into the nose. The mucous membrane, a sticky wet layer covering the inner surfaces of the body, traps many organisms.

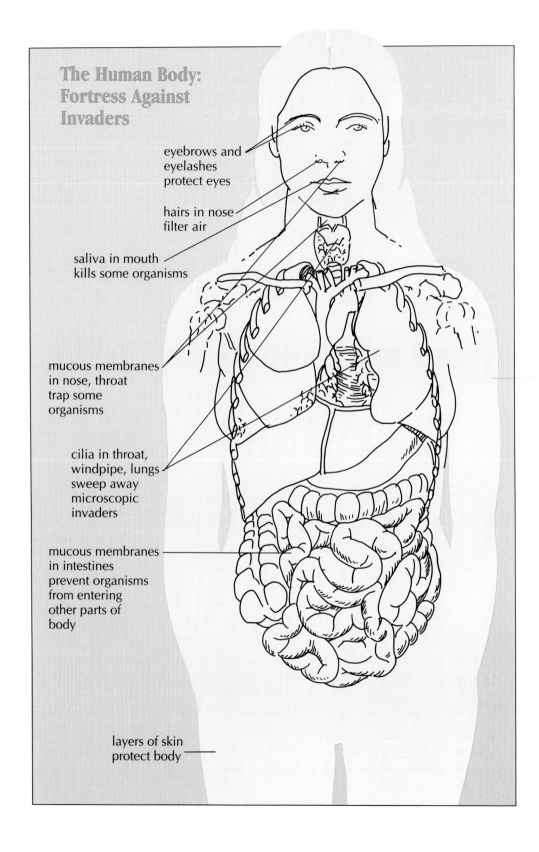

The Human Body: Fortress Against Invaders

eyebrows and
eyelashes
protect eyes

hairs in nose
filter air

saliva in mouth
kills some organisms

mucous membranes
in nose, throat
trap some
organisms

cilia in throat,
windpipe, lungs
sweep away
microscopic
invaders

mucous membranes
in intestines
prevent organisms
from entering
other parts of
body

layers of skin
protect body

Within the throat, windpipe, and lungs, tiny hairlike structures called cilia sweep microscopic invaders out of the body. Saliva in the mouth and fluid in the stomach contain substances that kill some organisms. Our intestines normally contain organisms that help with digestion. The mucous membrane of the intestines keeps these organisms from entering other parts of the body, where they could do harm.

There are certain organisms that manage to avoid the body's first line of defense. Some may enter the body through a cut in the skin or may escape the cilia of a natural opening, such as the ear or the throat. Once inside someone's body, these "invaders" begin to feed on the body's cells, destroying them. This is called an infection. Alerted to the invasion by cell destruction, body chemicals open the pores of tiny blood vessels called capillaries. Fluids and defensive cells pour through the capillary walls into the area of the invasion.

Once the fluids and defensive cells arrive at the infection site, a battle begins. Special proteins (chemicals essential to all cells) cover the invaders, preventing them from further harming the body. The defensive cells attack the invaders, which fight back. Some of them produce chemicals that are poisonous to body cells. Many times, this battle takes place and is won with few signs that the infected person can detect.

In other cases, however, the struggle to fight the infection is huge, and the person feels sick. The dilation (enlargement) of blood vessels carrying defense supplies to the scene causes redness. The buildup of dead cells and disease organisms causes swelling and pain. Chills and fever, which occur in response to the harmful organisms, or invaders, cause bodily discomfort, too.

Infection can also make a person feel sick because certain parts of the body are prevented from functioning properly. Sometimes this happens when organisms feed on the body's cells. Usually, however, parts of the body begin to function improperly because of the effects of fighting the infection. Large amounts of fluid, dead organisms, and dead body cells are produced. In the lungs, these materials cause breathing problems. If large areas of the lungs are affected, a condition called pneumonia develops. In the intestines, the extra fluid produced while a person is battling infection may cause cramps and diarrhea. In an ear, the pressure from the extra fluid causes pain and can affect hearing.

If the body's defenses cannot overcome the disease organisms, the invaders may continue to spread through the body. Some may attack vital organs and even cause death. But if the body's ability to fight these harmful organisms is not weakened by lack of sleep, lack of proper food, exposure to very hot or cold weather, and worry or stress, most infections can, in time, be stopped—often with a doctor's help.

A doctor may prescribe medicines that kill certain disease organisms. Other medicines can counteract the effects of poisons made by the invading disease organisms. Medicines that ease the symptoms of pain and swelling and help organs function properly may also be given.

The mission of the Centers for Disease Control in Atlanta, Georgia, is to protect the nation's health against communicable diseases. The staff includes doctors, nurses, biologists, chemists, technicians, and computer and environmental experts. They study contagious diseases, learn what causes them, and determine what can be done to control them. Staff experts provide information on vaccines and general health issues and the assistance that is needed to stop the outbreak of communicable diseases. They also study the body's disease defenses, blood diseases, blood chemistry, and illnesses that are caused by the environment in places such as schools, offices, and factories.

While doctors have many ways to deal with the invaders, it is certainly better if a person doesn't get sick in the first place. One important way to protect against communicable diseases is to prevent disease organisms from invading parts of the environment. Public-health doctors and researchers investigate the sources of organisms in air, water, and food. As a result of their research, government officials pass health laws that regulate water and food treatment as well as the control of insects and animals that transmit disease. Information about prevention is also given—advice about washing hands after using the bathroom, covering the mouth while coughing, and refrigerating certain foods. These regulations and procedures help to keep the spread of disease organisms to a minimum.

In the chapters that follow, you will read about the different kinds of organisms that can make people sick. You will also learn how our bodies and our doctors deal with these diseases in order to restore our health.

An electron microscope shows the *streptococcus pneumonae* bacteria that can cause pneumonia in humans.

3

Bacteria:
The Toxin Makers

Bacteria are tiny one-celled organisms that are neither animals nor plants. They belong to a third classification of life commonly known as Monera. Bacteria are all around us—in the air, in the soil, in the water, and on everything we touch. They are in our mouths, noses, throats, and intestines and on our skin and sex organs. Some bacteria are disease-causing organisms, but most are not capable of making us sick.

Many bacteria in our bodies are kept from multiplying and causing disease by our body's natural resistance. We can become resistant to a disease after we have been exposed to the bacterium that causes it. But when a disease-causing bacterium to which our body has not been previously exposed invades our body, the chances are much greater that it will make us sick.

Kelly, from Chapter 1, probably had strep throat in the past. After she recovered, some of the strep organisms remained in her throat. They didn't make her sick, but when she and Jeremy kissed, the organisms were passed on to Jeremy. His body had not been previously exposed to the organism, so he got sick. If Kelly's resistance is lowered because, for example, she doesn't eat properly or get enough rest, the organisms living in her throat may multiply and make her sick once again.

One major element of the body's resistance to bacterial diseases is a protein called an antibody. Antibodies are specific for different kinds of organisms. The body makes them in response to contact with foreign organisms (antigens). When an antigen enters your body, the body makes antibodies specifically for that organism. The body's ability to do this is the basis of immunization. To be immunized, a doctor injects a small amount of an organism, or parts of an organism, into your body. The organism has been treated so that it won't make you sick, but it does cause your body to make an antibody to fight the organism. Immunization spares you the risk of having to get the disease in order to make antibodies.

Antibodies work together with two kinds of white blood cells to fight disease organisms. Antibodies coat the disease organisms, making them targets for one kind of white blood cell, called a neutrophil, which swallows the disease organisms. The other kind of white blood cell, called a lymphocyte, makes new supplies of antibodies. In addition, the body makes a substance called complement that attacks the bacteria.

How Antibodies Work

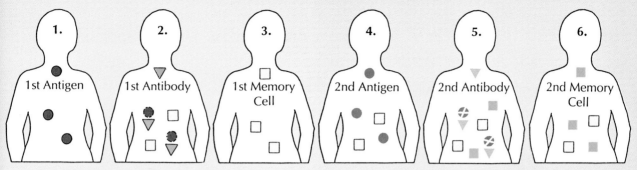

1. When an antigen (●) enters the bloodstream, it stimulates certain B lymphocytes to divide into plasma cells (▽) and memory cells (▢). **2.** Plasma cells secrete large amounts of a specific antibody, which circulates through the bloodstream and destroys the antigens. **3.** After their work is done, the antibodies disappear, leaving memory cells in circulation. These memory cells are sensitized to the antigen that was previously destroyed and will produce more antibodies if the antigen is detected again. This is the basis of long-term immunity. **4.** If a second, or new, antigen is detected, the initial process must begin again. **5.** New antibodies and memory cells are produced; the new antibodies destroy the new antigens. **6.** New memory cells remain in circulation, sensitized to the new (second) antigen.

A doctor's best weapon against bacterial infection is usually an antibiotic. Antibiotics are chemicals that kill bacteria by dissolving their cell walls or by destroying their ability to use nutrients (substances that provide nourishment for the body). Before a doctor can decide on the kind of antibiotic to give, the bacterium causing the infection must be identified. Usually, a doctor takes a sample from the infected area of the person and looks at it under a microscope. The doctor may also send a sample to the laboratory for further examination. Once the bacterium is identified, the doctor prescribes for the patient an antibiotic designed to kill that particular organism. But, sometimes, the organism has inherited a resistance, and the doctor must try another antibiotic.

Bacteria defend themselves by producing chemicals called toxins. Toxins attack white blood cells, muscle cells, nerve cells, skin cells, and the heart. A doctor may give a patient antitoxins to counteract these effects.

Bacteria:
The Toxin
Makers

Cocci

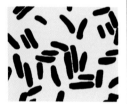

Bacilli

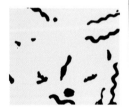

Spirilla

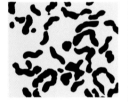

Vibrios

There are four basic kinds of bacteria—cocci, which have a round shape; bacilli, which are rod-shaped; spirilla, which have a spiral shape; and vibrios, which are curved. These bacteria are opportunists and can cause a wide variety of diseases. They produce disease when there is lowered resistance in the body or access to particular areas of the body. The following diseases are commonly caused by bacterial organisms, but many of these bacteria can cause other diseases.

Respiratory Contact

Some bacterial disease organisms are transmitted by droplets of saliva sneezed or coughed out by one person and then breathed in by another. Respiratory infections can also be transmitted by contact with an object such as a facial tissue or a drinking glass touched by the nose or mouth of an infected person. Some common respiratory infections are described here.

Strep throat is a type of sore throat. The symptoms of the disease, besides a sore throat, are fever, chills, headache, stomach ache, and a bright red tongue. If a red rash also develops on parts of the body, then the person is said to have scarlet fever.

Meningitis is a serious but rare infection of the covering of the brain and spinal cord. The infected person feels feverish, has a severe headache and stiff neck, and is very sensitive to light. Soon, vomiting begins, and the person becomes drowsy, then unconscious. Many people develop a red rash. Meningitis is usually the result of the spread of an infection from the throat, ear, or the sinuses. Since the disease attacks the outer surfaces of the brain, a recovered patient may be left with some brain damage, but this depends on which area of the brain was affected. A less serious kind of meningitis is caused by an organism called a virus, which you will read about in the next chapter.

Pneumonia is an infection of the lungs. It usually follows a less serious infection, such as a cold. When the organisms invade the lungs, fluid fills parts of the lungs, and the person develops a fever and has difficulty breathing. Coughing produces a yellow, blood-streaked fluid called mucus. Pneumonia is often caused by viruses, but bacteria may also cause it. There is a vaccine for pneumococcal pneumonia, a bacterial type of pneumonia, but none for the virus.

Whooping cough is an infection of the windpipe, or trachea, and the main passageways in the lungs, called bronchi. The infection starts with the symptoms of a cold—cough, sneezing, runny nose, fever, sore eyes. Then a more severe cough develops. As the person struggles to inhale between coughs, he or she makes a whooping sound. Violent coughing sometimes causes vomiting. A vaccination given to babies has made whooping cough a rare disease.

Diphtheria is an infection that begins in a person's throat, where the outer layer of cells in the throat are destroyed. The throat reacts by oozing a fluid, which forms a tough skin or scab over the throat area, making it difficult for the person to breathe. Diphtheria can also cause damage to the heart and other parts of the body.

Because it can be prevented by vaccination, this once-dangerous disease is now uncommon.

Tuberculosis is caused by a bacterial organism that infects the lungs. The organism, however, may remain in the lungs for years before it produces infection. One third of the world's population is believed to carry the organism; 10 to 15 million are Americans. A person carrying the organism has a lowered resistance and can therefore get the disease. The infected person develops a cough, chest pain, and fever; starts sweating; has trouble breathing; and loses weight. Eventually, the damage to the lungs can lead to death. Tuberculosis is transmitted to another person when an infected person coughs the organism into the air. One contact with the organism can be enough for a person to become infected. Though the disease was once the leading cause of death in the United States, antibiotics that killed the organism were discovered in the 1940s. A vaccine was also developed.

Today the number of tuberculosis victims in the United States is

The Attack of Tuberculosis

ingested
inhaled
in bloodstream
throat
lung
heart
kidney
intestines

Inhaled tuberculosis bacteria produces lesions in the lungs. It can infect the lymph nodes and enter the bloodstream, spreading to organs such as the kidneys. Ingested bacteria can infect the throat and intestines.

growing. The cause is believed to be lowered resistance to the disease. Drug abuse, homelessness, and poverty can cause malnutrition, which severely lowers resistance. AIDS also lowers resistance. Medicine to cure tuberculosis must be taken for long periods of time. If a person takes the medicine for too short a time, the organism becomes resistant to the medicine, and there is no way to kill it. When this organism is passed on, those who are infected by it cannot receive treatment either. The original organism's resistance has made it impossible for anyone to fight it with antibiotics.

Contamination of Food and Water by Feces

There are some bacteria that are transmitted from feces—bodily waste that forms in the large intestine—to food through water that has been contaminated (made impure) by flies or the soiled hands of food preparers. Drinking water contaminated with feces can also cause bacterial infection.

Typhoid fever is an intestinal infection. Symptoms include headache, fever, appetite loss, fatigue, stomach pain, and constipation, followed by diarrhea and the development of tiny red spots on the skin of the stomach and chest. Unless treated with antibiotics, the organisms will cause internal bleeding and the spread of the infection to other parts of the body, which can lead to death. Typhoid is not a problem in the United States or many other countries because of water-purification systems. People traveling to underdeveloped countries are immunized against typhoid.

Bacillary dysentery is a bacterial infection that attacks the walls of the intestines. Symptoms include fever, vomiting, cramps, and bloody diarrhea. Most often, antibiotics are used to stop the infection.

Insect Bites

Insects pass some disease organisms from animals to other animals or to people.

Lyme disease is transmitted by the bite of a bacteria-infected tick, a small bloodsucking animal, that normally infests deer. A red dot appears on the body where a

The tell-tale sign of Lyme disease appears on the arm of an adult male who was bitten by a Lyme tick.

Lyme tick bite occurred. This dot develops into an inch-wide bull's-eye—a red dot with a red ring around it. The person then develops a fever, headache, and muscle pains and feels tired, as if he or she had the flu. Redness and swelling of the knees, elbows, hips, and shoulders follow. Numbness and tingling in different parts of the body, double vision, and loss of the sense of taste may also occur. Antibiotics will cure the disease, but there is no way to immunize against it. The best way to prevent it is to prevent exposure to ticks.

Typhus is caused by a bacteria-like organism that lives inside the cells of other organisms. The organism is transmitted from rats to humans by the bite of a small bloodsucking insect called a louse (plural, *lice*). The infected person develops a headache, backache, high fever, and rash. The organism invades the blood vessels of most of the major organs of the body. The person dies when the heart, lungs, or kidneys fail. Typhus can be treated with antibiotics, and killing the lice controls the disease. Murine typhus, spread from rats to people by fleas, and Rocky Mountain spotted fever, spread from small animals to people by ticks, are similar infections.

Direct Contact

Some bacterial disease organisms are transmitted by direct, body-to-body contact between humans or animals.

Gonorrhea is a venereal disease, which means that it is transmitted during sexual intercourse. The most common symptoms for men are pain during urination and the discharge of a thick, yellow mucus from the penis. The infection can spread to other nearby organs, including the bladder and the prostate, a gland at the base of the bladder. The first symptom of gonorrhea for women is a mild irritation of the urethra, or urinary canal. An invasion of the female sex organs and the pelvic area follows. The infection may get into the bloodstream and can infect the joints and the heart. Damage to the sex organs may make a person sterile (unable to have children). Since the body does not make antibodies to fight the organism, people can get the infection many times. The bacteria, however, can be killed by certain medicines.

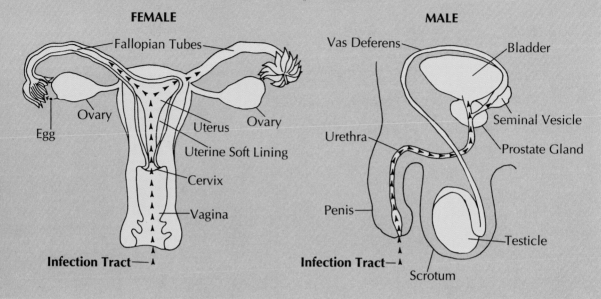

FEMALE

Fallopian Tubes

Ovary

Egg

Uterus   Ovary

Uterine Soft Lining

Cervix

Vagina

Infection Tract

MALE

Vas Deferens

Bladder

Seminal Vesicle

Urethra

Prostate Gland

Penis

Testicle

Infection Tract

Scrotum

Chlamydia is a sexually transmitted disease that causes symptoms similar to those of gonorrhea. It is the most common venereal disease in the United States and can cause a woman to become sterile even though the symptoms are often not obvious in women. Scarring produced by chlamydia is believed to be the major cause of ectopic pregnancy, a dangerous condition in which an embryo develops in one of the fallopian tubes (thin tubes leading from the ovaries to the uterus) instead of the uterus. Antibiotics will treat chlamydia.

Syphilis is a venereal disease that begins as a small open sore near the sex organs, the anus, or the mouth. The sore goes away after a month or so, but a skin rash, headaches, pain in the bones, and fever then develop. Hair may also begin to fall out. Without antibiotics, syphilis may damage the bones, tongue, heart, arteries, and brain and, in time, will certainly cause death.

Tularemia is an infection caused by a bacterium and is transmitted by contact with infected animals such as squirrels and rabbits. It begins with a red, open sore at the point of contact. Then the person develops fever, weakness, headache, and muscle pains. The infection can invade the liver, lungs, eyes, and other parts of the body. Humans can get tularemia from the bite of an infected tick, flea, fly, or louse or from eating under-cooked flesh of an infected animal. Since most people in the United States get the disease from rabbits which are often pets, a rabbit that looks sick should never be touched. Tularemia is most often effectively treated with antibiotics.

French chemist Louis Pasteur developed a method to prevent the transmission of certain dangerous bacteria found in milk. The process, called pasteurization, kills the bacteria by heating the milk to about 72° F.

Transmitted by Milk

Several harmful bacteria are passed on from infected cows into their milk. If infected milk is drunk by humans or other animals, it can cause various problems, some of which can be very serious.

Brucellosis is transmitted from animals to humans by milk or by the handling of infected animals. Symptoms include a high fever, aching, chills, swelling and backache. The disease can lead to other serious problems, like pneumonia and meningitis. Pasteurizing milk (heating it to a certain temperature) removes any possibility of a person getting brucellosis from milk.

This microscopic enlargement shows an AIDS virus (blue) attacking a human white blood cell, which helps the body fight infection.

4

Viruses: The Cell Invaders

Viruses are not alive. Living organisms can digest food,
use oxygen, grow, and reproduce themselves. Viruses
can do none of these things on their own. They are
particles, shaped like balls or rods, many times smaller
than bacteria. A single virus particle consists of an inner
core of chemicals called nucleic acids surrounded by
one or two protective shells made up of protein. The
nucleic acids—ribonucleic acid (RNA) and deoxyribo-
nucleic acid (DNA)—are the same type of chemicals
that make up the hereditary material, or genes, in our
cells and the cells of all other living organisms. The
genes we inherit from our parents control the activities
of our cells by controlling the production of different
kinds of proteins and other chemicals.

   Viruses can take on one important quality of life—
that of reproduction—when they invade living cells.

Once inside, a virus particle takes over operation of the cell. Viral nucleic acids direct the cell to make the nucleic acids and the protein that the virus needs to make more virus particles. In a few hours, one virus particle can produce 100 or more particles just like itself. The viral particles pour out of the cell and get into other cells. Usually, the invaded cells are destroyed by the virus. Viral particles have certain target cells, those that are particularly sensitive to their invasion. Some may invade lung cells, others may invade nerve cells, and still others may invade liver cells.

The invasion of the body's cells by viral particles is called a viral infection. If the particles remain in the area, they cause what is called a local infection, like a wart. If the particles reach the bloodstream, the person will have the typical signs of a systemwide, or systemic, infection—fever, headache, tiredness, achiness. From the bloodstream, the virus particles may then invade other parts of the body, producing symptoms of specific viral infections. Damage to liver cells may cause jaundice, a yellowing of the skin and whites of the eyes, typical of hepatitis and other liver diseases. Damage to certain nerve cells may cause paralysis (a condition in which the person cannot move certain parts of the body). Viruses, unlike bacteria, do not make toxins that poison the body. But what is left from the destruction of thousands of cells can poison many vital body organs, such as the heart or brain.

The body mounts a defense against invading viral particles. The entrance of the particles activates the body's immune system. Lymphocytes—white blood cells—destroy the particles. Antibodies assist the white blood cells by making the virus particles more sensitive to attack. Antibodies also affect the virus particles by hampering their ability to enter cells. Cells invaded by virus particles produce a protein called interferon, which helps to protect other cells from viruses.

A doctor cannot do much to help an infected person's immune system kill a virus. Viruses live in the cells, so any medicine that would kill the virus would also kill the cells. There are, however, several medicines that treat viral infection well—some can even prevent viruses from invading cells. A few, such as interferon that is produced in a laboratory, can also prevent viruses from multiplying.

Once a person has recovered from an infection, he or she is most often immune to that disease because the body has made a supply of antibodies for that virus. Doctors can prevent the infection in the first place by administering a vaccination that causes the body to make antibodies. The antibodies produced by the vaccination will stop the virus in its tracks. But antibodies are specific, so those for yellow fever, for example, will not fight a measles virus. A person needs a vaccination against each kind of viral infection. Viruses can change, or mutate, as they multiply. This means that the antibody made as a result of the vaccination for the original virus may not attack a mutant, or changed, virus. Flu viruses mutate on a regular basis, which is why with each new epidemic a flu shot is needed.

Viruses can be transmitted in much the same way as bacteria. The following are examples of viral infections transmitted by way of the air, food contaminated by feces, animal or insect bites, and direct contact.

Viruses in the Air

Virus particles can be transmitted when one person coughs or sneezes them into the air and another person inhales them. Viruses can also be transmitted when a person touches an object contaminated by a virus.

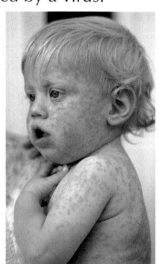

Measles is caused by a virus that invades the throat, the covering of the eye, or the skin. Frequently the infection begins with a fever, runny eyes and nose, and a cough. Bluish-white spots surrounded by a raised pink area appear inside the mouth. A person then develops a rash behind the ears. The rash spreads across the forehead, down the face, and over the rest of the body. By the time the rash reaches the feet, the patient is starting to feel better, but the infection can later spread to the lungs, the ears, and the brain. There is an effective vaccine for measles.

Rubella, or **German measles,** is similar to measles, but it is milder. The infection is more serious for adults than for children. If a pregnant woman gets the disease, her baby may be born with defects such as deafness or mental retardation. There is a vaccination for rubella.

Chicken pox is caused by a virus that invades the skin and throat cells. The person develops a slight fever and a rash inside the mouth, throat, and on the skin. Chicken pox is a mild infection for children, but it can bring on pneumonia and other serious problems in adults. A vaccine for chicken pox is not commonly used in the United States, and the virus may remain in the body after the person gets well. Years later, the virus may invade the nerves in the chest wall and the skin of the neck and the head. This infection is called shingles. Symptoms of shingles include severe pain and paralysis.

Fecal Contamination of Food and Water

Some viral diseases are transmitted when food or water is contaminated by feces.

Polio is mainly transmitted in feces, but it can also be transmitted through the air. It is caused by a virus that invades the throat, the intestines, and the nerve cells.

American microbiologist Jonas Salk developed the first effective polio vaccine in 1953.

Symptoms include fever, sore throat, headache, and vomiting. These symptoms usually go away after a few days, but sometimes the headache gets worse, the neck and back become stiff, and the muscles ache and twitch. Some of a victim's muscles may become permanently paralyzed and if the brain is affected, the person may die. A vaccine prevents the disease.

Infectious hepatitis, or **viral hepatitis type A,** is caused by a virus that invades the cells of the liver, the body's main chemical factory. The liver makes proteins that fight infection and help the blood to clot. The liver also changes raw materials into nutrients that the body can use and it removes poisons from the blood. The liver also makes bile, which helps the intestines digest fats. Liver disease can affect many vital body functions. Symptoms of liver infection include tiredness, achiness, vomiting, fever, and loss of appetite. Pain in the upper part of the abdomen, where the liver is, may follow. An infected person's skin and eyes may get jaundiced, or yellow, which indicates that the liver has not been cleaning the blood well enough. Doctors generally treat hepatitis patients with a diet that is rich in sugar and low in fat. Infectious hepatitis can be controlled by proper sanitation procedures that help to prevent fecal contamination of food and water. A vaccine for hepatitis A has just recently been developed.

Viruses and Animal Bites

Rabies is caused by a virus that invades the nerve cells and the salivary glands (glands that produce saliva in the mouth). It can be transmitted from an animal to a human in one of two ways. The animal's saliva can enter a person's bloodstream by means of a bite or break in the person's skin. Symptoms of the infection include fever, tiredness, sore throat, headache, and loss of appetite. The area where the virus entered the skin begins to itch, and light, noise, and touch bother the person. Muscles begin to twitch, and the mouth fills with large amounts of saliva.

Raccoons are common carriers of rabies.

Sweating begins, and then the muscles of the face and throat become paralyzed. Paralysis spreads, and the patient soon dies. It is not possible to save a rabies victim once the infection begins, which is usually four to eight weeks after the virus enters the body. The best procedure is to immediately give a person a vaccine if he or she has been bitten by a rabid animal. In the United States, raccoons and skunks are among the most common animals that transmit rabies. Since animals often give the virus to each other through bites, pets can also get the disease. Vaccination of pets that may come in contact with wild animals is the best way to protect people from the disease.

Yellow fever is caused by a virus that invades the cells of the liver. It is transmitted from monkeys to humans or from one human to another by the bite of several types of mosquitoes found in the tropics. The infection can be mild, with symptoms such as headache, fever, achiness, and nausea (sickness at the stomach). More serious yellow-fever infections produce liver damage, signaled by yellowing of the skin. Bleeding in the stomach may also occur, and a person may vomit the digested blood, producing the "black vomit" that was once the name of the disease. Gums may bleed, and there may be bleeding in the brain, causing death. There is a vaccine for yellow fever, and control of the disease-carrying mosquito population also helps to prevent the disease from spreading.

Direct Contact with Viruses

There are some viral diseases that are spread by direct, person-to-person contact.

AIDS (acquired immune deficiency syndrome) is caused by HIV (human immunodeficiency virus). The virus can be transmitted during sexual relations, through needle sharing by drug addicts, through contaminated blood transfusions, and from an infected mother to her baby. The virus invades white blood cells known as T-4 lymphocytes, which control the response of the body to infectious disease. When T-4 lymphocytes are destroyed, the body becomes nearly defenseless against infection. It may take several years for the body's immune system to be destroyed, and during this time, the only sign of the disease is the swelling of tiny glands called lymph nodes. Lymph nodes capture and destroy infectious organisms and particles. Lymph nodes are located in the chest, abdomen, groin, and neck. Once the AIDS virus has destroyed the body's immune system, the person will get multiple infections, particularly of the mouth, tongue, lungs, eyes, and intestines. A kind of skin cancer linked to low immunity produces small bluish-red tumors on the legs and arms. While the local infections can be treated with antibiotics, there is no way to kill the AIDS virus. A drug called AZT does block the multiplication of the virus for a while, but it can also cause a low red-blood-cell count—anemia—and can interfere with the action of the antibiotics given to fight the other infections. There is no proven vaccine for AIDS, and most people die of the infection. However, a vaccine has been developed for a kind of leukemia that strikes cats. The virus that causes this disease is very similar to the AIDS virus, bringing hope that an AIDS vaccine will be developed soon. AIDS can often be prevented by the use of a condom during sexual relations, by sterilizing all needles used to puncture the skin, and by careful examination of all blood donors.

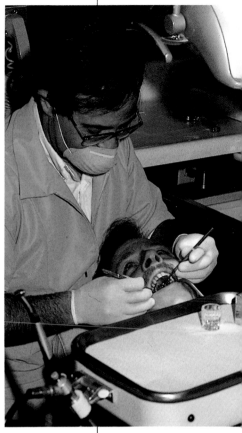

Because AIDS has reached epidemic proportions, many precautions are being taken. Doctors, nurses, and dentists are just a few of the health professionals who now commonly wear masks and gloves during contact with patients.

Viral hepatitis type B is passed from one person to another by exposure to the virus in the bloodstream. One method of transmission is through sexual contact (mainly among males who engage in unprotected anal sex). The virus is also transmitted from one person to another by contaminated blood transfusions, by needles shared by drug addicts, by shared razors, and by contaminated equipment used for piercing ears or tattooing skin. Symptoms include fever, achiness, tiredness, vomiting, and appetite loss. There is a vaccine for hepatitis B, and prevention involves the use of a condom during sexual contact, careful screening of blood donors, and the use of sterile needles and other skin-puncturing equipment.

Mouth and genital sores are caused by two forms of herpes virus. The cold-sore virus, or herpes simplex, is transmitted during direct contact with the lips. It invades the skin around the mouth, and blisters form on the lips or face. They disappear in about a week, but the virus remains in the cells. A fever or exposure to the sun may cause the blisters to return. The same type of virus produces genital herpes, which occurs as a painful blistering around the sex organs. It is transmitted during sexual intercourse and can be treated with medication.

There are two kinds of herpes virus that cause sores. One is sexually transmitted, and the other—herpes simplex—causes the cold sores that appear around the mouth.

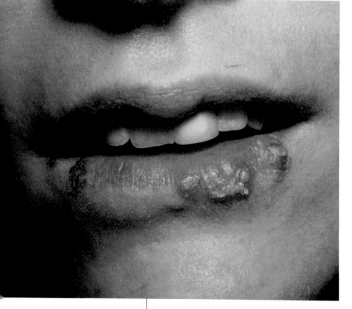

An Infectious Disease Is Conquered

Edward Jenner

In 1796, Edward Jenner, a well-known British doctor who had been researching communicable diseases, tested one of his observations. He had noticed that people who got cowpox did not get smallpox. Smallpox is a viral disease that causes blisters and pocks on the skin. Cowpox is a mild disease that dairy workers often caught from cows. Jenner obtained a sample from the pock of a cowpox victim and scratched it into the arm of an eight-year-old boy. After testing the boy, Jenner found that he was immune to smallpox. This was the first vaccination.

Over the years, vaccination greatly reduced the number of smallpox infections. By 1959, smallpox had been eliminated from Europe, North America, and parts of South America. A dream was born in the United Nations. Why not start a project to eliminate smallpox from the world? Since only humans could get smallpox, making all humans immune to the disease would stop the virus from causing infection. It was an awesome task. The citizens of 50 countries in South America, Asia, and Africa still ran the risk of getting smallpox.

Laboratories for making the vaccine were set up in each country. Vaccination teams from each country were trained and sent out to different parts of the world. Working with maps and local guides, they went into each village and town and vaccinated everyone they could find. A reporting system in each country kept the teams informed about areas where there were smallpox outbreaks. The teams were rushed to badly infected areas, where they vaccinated all those who were not infected. Then the area would be quarantined (closed to outsiders) to prevent the spread of the infection out of the area. The vaccination and quarantine effort went so well that soon the teams were working on very small outbreaks. Finally, as there were fewer and fewer cases, a new plan was put into effect. A village-by-village, house-by-house search for smallpox cases began. By 1977, the very last case of smallpox had been identified—it infected a man living in the African country of Somalia.

This magnified photo shows the head and neck of a tapeworm inside a human intestine. People commonly get tapeworm from eating raw or undercooked beef.

5

Fungi and Parasites

Fungi are tiny nongreen plants, most of which are either harmless or beneficial to humans. Some, however, can cause disease. These disease-causing fungi are essentially parasites—organisms that live in or on another organism—as are bacteria and viruses, which we have already discussed.

Fungi
There are about 100,000 kinds of fungi. They live in the soil, but the wind blows them all over. You have most likely seen them in a number of familiar places. That mildew on the shower curtain, that mold on the bread, that mushroom on the lawn—they are all fungi.

   A fungus, unlike most other plants, does not have chlorophyll, which is the chemical responsible for photosynthesis. Photosynthesis is the process that plants use to make their own sugars, starches, and other foods. Because it cannot make its own food, a fungus uses the food made by other forms of life. In fact, a fungus can feed on many familiar things, like cloth, animal feces, ink, food containers, glue, and paint.

Many fungi are useful to humans. The unique ability of fungi to digest just about anything is commonly used by food and beverage manufacturers to kill off bacteria. Fungi also help to make certain kinds of cheese. And yeast, a fungus, is used to make bread, beer, and wine. Some fungi make chemicals that kill disease bacteria. These chemicals are called antibiotics.

To invade and digest food, a fungus uses a branching structure called a mycelium. The mycelium grows from a spore, or seed, carried in the air. When the spore lands on a place where there is food, it begins to grow. It sprouts an extension, then another, forming a simple twiglike structure, called a hypha. The hypha sprouts into the branchlike mycelium, which makes new branches, extending and digesting food as it grows.

Mycelia also make spores that are carried to new areas, where they form other mycelia. Spores are thus the form in which fungi are transmitted. Many fungi can live only in certain areas under certain conditions of temperature and moisture. When a spore lands on a suitable plant or animal and begins to form a mycelium, this is called a fungal infection, or a mycosis. While fungi are responsible for many common plant and animal diseases, they cause very few human diseases.

Human fungal diseases often occur when a spore blown by the wind is inhaled, causing a serious lung infection. Sometimes a spore in the soil enters a cut or a wound. But these are not communicable diseases, because they are not passed from one person to another or from an animal to a person.

Local Fungal Infections

Local fungal diseases infect the skin, nails, and hair. They are caused by a group of fungi that are transmitted from one person to another through direct contact with contaminated materials.

Ringworm of the scalp affects both the hair and the scalp. Patches of hair break off, leaving bald spots on the head. The infection is passed from person to person by way of hair fragments on bedding, combs, clothing and upholstered furniture. It can also be passed on to people from cats and dogs.

Ringworm of the skin occurs on nonhairy parts of the body. The skin develops a round patch, of which the inner part is scaly and dry. The outer area is red and blistered. The fungus is transmitted either through person-to-person or animal-to-person contact.

Athlete's foot is an infection of the skin between the toes that causes itching, redness, and blisters. When the blisters break—releasing a thin fluid—the skin starts to peel, and painful cracks develop. This infection is transmitted from person to person on wet floors.

Jock itch is an infection most common among men. It begins in the genital area and then spreads to the thighs, causing redness and itching. Direct contact with a contaminated person or object transmits this fungus.

Fungus nail can attack the nails of the hands or the feet. The nails become thick and discolored, and the infection may also affect the toes or fingers and the skin surrounding them. Fungus nail is usually transmitted to the toes in showers, but it can also be transmitted to the fingers during manicures and during the application of artificial nails. The removal of the cuticle provides an entry for the fungus.

These local infections do not trigger a bodywide immune response. Because of this, the body does not make antibodies, and people can get the infections many times. A number of drugs have been developed to kill these fungi, but these drugs work slowly. People may need to take them for months or years.

Internal Fungal Infections

Some fungal infections are transmitted when spores, which are released into the soil by animal droppings, are blown by the wind and then inhaled. The body reacts to these infections by making antibodies. Once the person has recovered from the infection, he or she is immune.

Histoplasmosis infects the lungs and is transmitted by spores from bird or bat droppings. The infected person develops fever, aches and pains, coughing, and sometimes diarrhea. For most people, the infection is so mild that it is never noticed. For people such as AIDS patients, whose immunity is low, histoplasmosis can be very serious. The infection spreads to many parts of the body, and areas of major organs are destroyed. It can be fatal if it is not treated with medicine.

Fungal meningitis is a rare infection caused by an organism that is transmitted from soil contaminated with pigeon droppings and usually begins as a skin infection. Then, blisters, boils, and ulcers appear on the skin, and the infection spreads to the brain, causing a headache, a stiff neck, sensitivity to light, and vomiting. In some cases, the fungus can spread to the lungs. Medicine is used to stop the infection.

Sporotrichosis can be transmitted to people from infected animals (dogs, rats, horses, and mules) and from a number of plants. Transmission is through a break in the skin, producing small nodes, or lumps, under the skin. In most cases, it is a mild infection that is easily treated. The organism, however, may spread to the lungs of people whose immunity is low.

Parasites

A parasite is an organism that grows and feeds on another organism called a host. A host is harmed by a parasite. The two parasites that we will discuss here are protozoa and worms. While there are many kinds of protozoa and worms, only a few are parasites.

Protozoa are one-celled animals. They are so tiny that

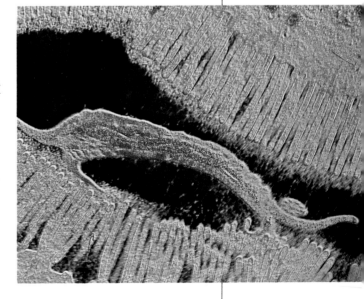

A microscopic parasite—enlarged more than 1,200 times—attaches itself to the wall of a human intestine. Many kinds of parasites are transmitted through food and water.

they can be seen only through a microscope. Worms are many-celled animals visible to the naked eye. There are several types of parasitic worms—flatworms, round-worms, and thorny-headed worms.

To understand how parasites are transmitted, it is important to know their life cycles. Most protozoa reproduce by splitting in half. Some go into a resting stage and cover themselves with a protective outer skin, called a cyst. The cyst leaves the host's body, usually in the feces. As a cyst, the protozoan is protected until it has the opportunity to enter another host. There, it develops into another adult. The malaria parasite, one of the protozoa, is an exception. Its life cycle is more like that of a worm.

Worms, like many animals, develop from eggs, which are also called ova (ovum for just one egg). The ova develop into adult forms. In most cases, there is a middle, wormlike form called a larva. Worms some-times have two hosts. Ova can change into larvae in one host. Later, the larvae are passed on to another host, where they develop into adults that produce ova.

Parasites have developed certain features that help them invade and live in the bodies of their hosts. Many parasite larvae can actually pierce the flesh of a host. They can do this because their bodies make proteins that digest skin. Some adults produce ova that can resist harsh outdoor conditions such as dryness, cold, and heat until they are swallowed by the host.

Parasites may enter humans as adults, eggs, or larvae. They are transmitted through direct contact with

How Protozoa Reproduce

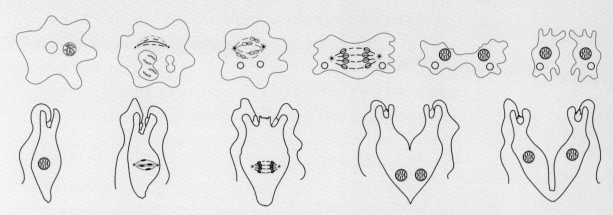

Protozoans multiply in a process called binary fission. In this process, one cell splits into two "daughter" cells. *Top*: The chromosomes in the nucleus of an amoeba separate. As the nucleus divides, the cell stretches and constricts in the middle to help the two daughter cells pull apart. *Bottom*: Euglena reproduce themselves by splitting down the middle from front to back and forming two equal cells. As the cell splits, the nucleus divides and new organisms are formed.

contaminated hands, clothing, or through the skin. Some parasites are transmitted by the bite of an insect. Others may enter by way of the mouth when a person swallows water or food contaminated with feces that contain ova. In other cases, the food swallowed may be part of an animal whose body contains parasite larvae.

Once inside the body of a host, a parasite needs a way to remove food from the host. Some worms have hooks and suckers to attach themselves to the host's intestinal walls and suck its blood. Some protozoa and worm larvae make proteins that dissolve the intestinal walls and other parts of the body. Others invade red blood cells. The diet of the host seems to favor certain parasites. For example, some parasites seem to thrive in a person whose diet is rich in sugar and starch. A diet that is low in protein favors other parasites.

A parasite's efforts to multiply, to feed, and to move around in the host can often make the host sick. Larvae may get into muscles, the liver, and the brain and may affect the functioning of these organs. Adult parasites remove important nourishment from the host. Some kinds of adult parasites may actually clog areas such as the intestines and lungs.

The human body's immune system does produce antibodies against many parasites. In fighting these invaders, a person often becomes feverish, tired, and achy, usually at the beginning of a parasitic disease. There is no way to vaccinate against a parasite, but doctors do have medicines that kill parasites.

Public health parasite-control measures include carefully disposing of feces and other bodily wastes, purifying water, controlling insects that transmit parasites, thoroughly cooking the flesh of animals that may be hosts, and enforcing strict hygiene codes.

Some of the many diseases caused by parasitic protozoa and parasitic worms are described in the following section. The ways in which the diseases can be transmitted, the symptoms, and the treatment are explained.

Parasitic Protozoa

Parasitic protozoa can cause disease in a number of ways. A person can get infected by an insect bite, by direct contact with another person who is infected, or by swallowing contaminated food or water.

Malaria is transmitted by the bite of a mosquito that lives in tropical countries. The mosquito is infected when it bites a person who has malaria. Larvae then develop inside the mosquito. When the mosquito bites a second person, it infects that person's blood with the larvae. The larvae invade the liver of the person and multiply. Then they move out of the liver and into the person's red blood cells. The larvae mature in the red blood cells. There they destroy the cells as they escape into the bloodstream. This destruction occurs every other day. Chills, fever, and sweating accompany this. When another mosquito bites that person, it picks up some of the larvae in the bloodstream, and the cycle begins all over again. While malaria is considered a tropical disease, a person living in the United States is also at risk of getting it. Sometimes the disease is transmitted by a drug addict who shares a needle with a person who was infected with malaria in the tropics.

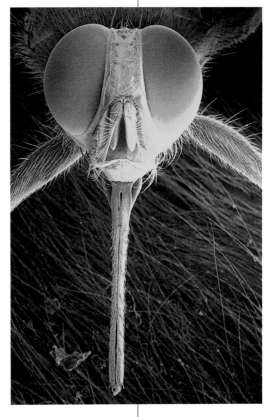

A protozoan parasite called *trypanosoma* incubates inside a tsetse fly, shown here. When the fly bites a human, the parasite is transmitted, causing sleeping sickness.

Sleeping sickness is spread from person to person by the bite of the tsetse fly, an insect that lives in Africa. Parasitic protozoa mature and reproduce inside the fly. In humans, the organisms invade the brain, eventually causing a person to appear to be asleep. Without medicine, the person will die.

Amebic dysentery is caused by a tiny organism that is transmitted from one person to another by eating food or drinking water contaminated with feces containing cysts. Cysts are coiled organisms that have a shell-like skin. When a person swallows them, the cysts change into mature organisms and move into the large intestine, where the organism produces a protein that dissolves a small part of the intestinal wall. It then begins to swallow the red blood cells, and the person develops stomach pains and diarrhea. In more severe cases, a person may develop a fever; stomach ulcers; and watery, bloody diarrhea. The organism may spread to the liver, the lungs, and the brain, sometimes causing permanent damage. Amebic dysentery is common in underdeveloped countries, where there are no sewage and water-treatment systems.

Toxoplasmosis is caused by a small crescent-shaped organism that invades the body's cells and multiplies in them. The organism usually infects pigs, lambs, cats, and people. A small percentage of cats pass the cysts in their feces. The parasite can be transmitted to people when they eat undercooked pork or lamb containing the cysts or when they handle cat feces. Most people are resistant to the infection, but it can cause a mild illness, similar to the flu, that infects parts of the eye. It is a dangerous illness for a pregnant woman because it may cause the baby to be stillborn (born dead). It is also a dangerous disease for people with low immunity, such as newborn babies and people with AIDS. In babies, toxoplasmosis can cause blindness, enlargement of the liver and spleen, and mental retardation. AIDS patients with toxoplasmosis can suffer severe damage to the brain, lungs, and heart.

Giardiasis is caused by a pear-shaped organism that infects the small intestine, causing diarrhea and pain. It sometimes invades the gall bladder, affecting a person's ability to digest fat. The parasites are passed out of the body as cysts in the feces. Giardiasis is mainly transmitted through fecal-contaminated food and water. However, the disease can also be transmitted by hand-to-mouth or sexual contact. In the past, giardiasis was only a problem in countries without sewage and water-treatment plants. But in recent years, the disease has struck people in the United States— preschool children, homosexual men, and those living in prisons, mental institutions, and nursing homes.

Dysentery and giardiasis can be transmitted through certain contaminated food and water supplies.

Parasitic Worms

Several infections caused by parasitic worms are transmitted to people by direct contact with a worm or by the bite of a worm. Others are caused by contaminated food and water, a problem in many areas with poor sewage, sanitation, and health codes. Lack of water purification, improper cooking techniques, and poor hygiene by food handlers also contribute to this problem.

Hookworm is caused by two kinds of thorny-headed worms that have bent-hooked heads and toothlike structures on each side of their heads. Hookworms are about a half-inch long. Their larvae live in the soil, pierce the skin of the feet, and travel to the small intestine where they grow into mature hookworms. Using their teeth, the hookworms attach themselves to a person's intestinal walls and feed on blood and other fluids. They produce ova that pass out into the soil with the feces. The ova change into larvae in the soil and infect other people. A person with hookworm feels slight pains in the stomach and may suffer from diarrhea and lung problems. But the biggest problem for the person is the loss of blood. In addition to prescribing medicine to kill the parasites, doctors may give the infected person blood transfusions or iron pills. Hookworm is a problem in countries with poor sanitation. It affects about 700 million people throughout the world.

Schistosomiasis is caused by flatworms known as flukes. A fluke is about an inch long. Fluke ova from human urine and feces can contaminate lakes and rivers, hatch into larvae, and enter the bodies of small snails in the water. Inside the snails, they change into more mature larvae. The larvae then leave the snail and return to the water, where they can pierce the skin of a person swimming or bathing. Once inside the body, the flukes change into adults and invade the intestines and bladder, where they lay their ova. The ova then pass out of the body and into the water by way of the urine and feces. When the bladder and intestines are invaded, blood gets into the urine or feces. The disease can cause serious damage to the liver, bladder, and kidneys. It occurs in tropical countries, where people use lakes and rivers for toilets. There is one kind of fluke that cannot infect people; it just causes itching, or *swimmer's itch*. As they move around in the water, the larvae of these flukes can get under a swimmer's skin. But they are unable to move inside the human body. The flukes soon die, leaving behind blisters and small bumps on the skin.

Pinworms are caused by roundworms that are about a third of an inch long. They commonly infect children all over the world. Pinworms live in the intestines and at night travel downward and out of the anus—the opening at the end of the large intestine. There, they lay their ova on the skin surrounding the anus. This causes itching, and when a person scratches the skin, the ova get on the hands. The ova are transmitted to other people through contact with clothing, toys, sheets, or air contaminated with the ova. Pinworms are easily treated.

Filariasis, or **elephantiasis,** is caused by threadlike roundworms that can be as long as 20 inches. The parasite is transmitted from person to person by the bite of several kinds of mosquitoes and flies that live in many Asian, European, Central American, and African nations. When an infected insect bites a person, the larvae pass into that person's body and invade the lymphatic system, where they then grow into adult worms. This system is similar to the blood-circulation system. It carries fluids and infection-fighting cells throughout the body. In the lymphatic system, the adult worms produce cysts containing larvae that pass into an insect's body when it bites an infected person. The insect then passes on the larvae to other people it bites. A victim develops an illness similar to the flu that lasts just a few days. If there are a lot of worms in a person's body, they irritate the lymphatic vessels, causing the legs to swell and the skin to become thick and dark. The swelling and thickened skin make the legs look like those of an elephant. The swelling can also affect the arms and the sex organs.

A worm similar to the one that causes filariasis invades the eye, causing blindness. This condition is called *river blindness* and is transmitted by a tiny black fly that lives near fast-flowing rivers in Africa and South America.

Tapeworms are flatworms that are transmitted when a person eats undercooked meat or fish containing cysts of the tapeworm larvae. The larvae develop into adult worms in the intestines and may grow to 20 or 30 feet. A tapeworm attaches itself to the intestinal wall by means of four suckers and hooks on its head. It then feeds on the intestinal fluids. The adult worms produce ova that are passed out of the intestine by means of the feces. Animals such as cows, pigs, and fish swallow the ova as they feed. The ova develop into cysts in the animal's muscles, and when a person eats the under-cooked, cured, or pickled flesh of an infected animal, he or she becomes infected. Except for some diarrhea, the person may not notice the invasion of the worm. The most dangerous effect of tapeworms occurs when the ova move upward out of the intestine and into the stomach, which causes a condition called *cysticercosis*. The ova can also develop into cysts in the muscles and the brain causing the infected person to experience muscle pain and convulsions (twitching and jerking).

Cysticercosis can also be caused by swallowing food that is contaminated with ova from the hands of a person who has tapeworm. There are several medicines that can be given to kill tapeworm.

Trichinosis is similar to tapeworm. A person gets the disease from eating undercooked pork or pork products, such as ham, that contain cysts of a certain roundworm. The roundworms, which are about two inches long, live in the intestines, where they produce larvae that invade the heart, muscles, and brain. Trichinosis is treated with a medicine that kills adult worms in the intestines and attacks larvae in the tissues.

Ascariasis is an infection that affects the small intestine. It is caused by a roundworm that is between 6 and 15 inches long and that resembles an earthworm. Its ova are transmitted when a person eats food grown in soil contaminated with feces from an infected person. While in the intestine, the ova hatch into larvae. They then travel through the intestinal walls, the blood, the lungs, and the windpipe, and return to the intestine. There they develop into adult worms that produce ova that pass out of the body in the feces. A mildly infected person usually has no symptoms or may just experience stomach pain. People infested with large amounts of worms can be robbed of nourishment and develop malnutrition. A roundworm is extremely active. If it is irritated by certain foods or medicine, it may leave the intestine and invade other parts of the body. When this happens, it causes many kinds of problems, depending on the part of the body it invades.

A laboratory technician inspects a device that screens anti-infectious agents. Modern science is constantly discovering new ways to battle our most serious health threats.

6

From the Laboratories: New Ideas for Fighting Disease

We have come a long way from the days when common communicable diseases killed person after person. A number of these diseases were easy to prevent or cure, but they were destructive because no one knew how they were spread.

Today, we know how many diseases are transmitted, so we are able to control them. In the majority of cases, the organisms that cause diseases have been identified. With that accomplished, it has been possible to make vaccines from those organisms after they have been killed or weakened. Once inside the body, the proteins on the outside walls of the organisms (the antigens) stimulate the body to produce antibodies. As we have learned, antibodies make people immune, or resistant, to infections.

But a new age of "designer" vaccines is beginning. We no longer need a scientist to conduct a long search for each proper antigen or organism for making each vaccine. Now, using complicated chemical techniques, scientists can simply create a vaccine from a "recipe" designed to fight a specific disease.

Already a new technique has produced two vaccines that are effective for treating hepatitis B. Medical scientists are using this technique to prepare vaccines for serious infections, including malaria, sleeping sickness, and even AIDS.

One new malaria vaccine would prevent the spread of the organism from humans to mosquitoes, where the organism matures. Preventing malaria organisms from maturing would eventually wipe out the disease. Still another malaria vaccine, which is about to be tested on humans, would kill the organism at several stages. A vaccine for malaria cannot come too soon. By the 1990s, doctors were beginning to notice that chloroquine, a medicine used to kill the malaria organism, was no longer working very well. The organism had become resistant to the medicine, and the malaria parasite was still thriving, striking hundreds of millions of people and killing several million each year.

Scientists today are also using a genetic approach to fight malaria's resistance to chloroquine. They are working to identify the gene in the organism that is responsible for chloroquine resistance. Then they hope to be able to stop the gene from working.

Sleeping sickness is a serious disease that affects people in Africa. It kills about 10,000 people a year—and it kills their herds of cattle. Scientists hope to change the genes of the organism in a way that would make it harmless. Then they will use that organism to make a vaccine.

Knowledge about the chemistry and the genetics of the AIDS virus has provided scientists with many ideas, not only for making vaccines, but also for killing the organism once it strikes. One idea involves placing proteins inside the person's cells that destroy the reproductive nucleic acids of the virus. Other ideas focus on the various stages of development of the virus inside the body. For example, some scientists are looking for a way to block the protein used by the virus to make its protective outer coat. Others are seeking ways to stop the virus's chemical control of its reproduction.

The discovery that molds made substances that killed bacteria was an accident, but it spurred the development of antibiotics. There is nothing accidental about the way antibiotics are discovered today. The reaction between an antibiotic and a disease organism is a kind of chemical lock-and-key bonding. If the antibiotic bonds properly with the chemicals on the surface of the disease organism, the antibiotic kills the disease.

Making an antibiotic begins in the laboratory. The chemical makeup of a disease organism is determined. Then a computer search is conducted for the correct "key," or chemical, that will bond with the chemicals on the surface of the organism. Once the key is discovered, the formula for the antibiotic can be created, and the new antibiotic is made in the laboratory. After testing to make sure the drug works and isn't harmful, it is ready to be used on the general population to fight infection.

Scientists are also at work on an idea for making substances similar to antibiotics that can kill disease organisms. One such substance has been discovered inside a disease-fighting white blood cell called a neutrophil. This cell swallows disease organisms and then destroys them. Scientists have discovered that the neutrophil uses a protein, called defensin, to kill disease organisms, and they have recently learned how to make defensin. In the test tube, researchers find that defensin is effective for killing disease organisms—as effective as antibiotics. Now defensin will have to be tested on animals and people.

The fight against disease has moved from the biology laboratory to the chemistry laboratory. Although research scientists have not come up with the means to prevent or cure all communicable diseases, the technology available to them provides great hope. With each day, scientists know a little bit more about how to approach the study of disease. And each day their knowledge brings the rest of the world closer to a day when all disease will be quickly and easily treated.

Development of new vaccines and drug treatments requires a great deal of time and money. Scientists often spend years searching for effective new drugs, and some are never found.

Glossary

anemia A condition in which a person lacks sufficient hemoglobin in the blood. Hemoglobin is the substance in the blood that carries oxygen.

antibiotic A human-made substance that kills bacteria.

antibody A protein produced by the body that fights infection.

antigen A protein, foreign to the body, that stimulates the production of infection-fighting substances in the body called antibodies.

antitoxin A substance that neutralizes the effects of toxins, or poisons.

bacilli Rod-shaped forms of bacteria.

bacteria Microscopic one-celled organisms.

capillaries Tiny blood vessels that connect the arteries and the veins.

chlorophyll The chemical in plant leaves used by the plant to make food by using light in a chemical process called photosynthesis.

chloroquine The drug used to kill the malaria organism.

cilia Tiny hairlike projections on the surface of certain living cells that move constantly, pushing out foreign materials such as bacteria, mucus, and dust.

cocci Spherical forms of bacteria.

complement A substance made by the body that kills bacteria.

cyst A microscopic organism covered with a protective outer skin.

defensin A protein that kills disease organisms.

feces Bodily waste that forms in the large intestine.

fungus A nongreen plant that does not undergo photosynthesis and cannot make its own food.

gene A unit of heredity that influences a special feature of an organism.

hepatitis An inflammation, or injury, of the liver caused by infection or chemicals.

herpes A virus disease of the skin in which tiny blisters form in clusters.

host An organism that shelters and feeds another organism called a parasite.

hypha Twiglike structures that form the body of a fungus.

immunization The process of making a person resistant to a disease by injecting disease organisms or antibodies.

infection A condition that occurs when disease organisms multiply within the body.

interferon A protein made by the body that interferes with the multiplication of viruses; also a drug produced in the laboratory.

jaundice Yellowing of the skin and the whites of the eyes most often caused by liver disease.

larva The intermediate form of the parasitic worm that develops from an ovum, or egg.

life cycle The cycle of development of an organism during which it becomes an adult and produces new organisms.

local infection An infection caused when a disease organism remains near its point of entry and does not enter the bloodstream.

lymphocyte A white blood cell that fights infection by attacking disease organisms and making disease-fighting proteins called antibodies.

mucous membrane The soft, pink, skinlike layer that lines many of the body's organs and passages, such as the nose and mouth, that lead to the outside.

mucus A thick, clear, sticky fluid found in the nose, mouth, and other passages and areas that open to the outside.

mutation A change in the genes within the cells, producing a change in the characteristics of the organism.

mycelium The branching body of a fungus.

mycosis An infection caused by a fungus.

neutrophil A white blood cell that fights infection by swallowing a disease organism and killing it.

nucleic acids Chemicals that make up genes, the hereditary material of an organism.

nutrient A substance that provides nourishment for the body.

ovum A female reproductive cell.

parasite An organism that lives on or in another organism.

photosynthesis The chemical process by which plants make food, using chlorophyll and the energy from the sun.

protein A chemical compound made up of carbon, hydrogen, nitrogen, and oxygen that is an essential part of every cell.

protozoa One-celled organisms.

spirilla Spiral-shaped forms of bacteria.

spores Seedlike forms produced by fungi.

sterile Unable to reproduce one's own kind.

symptom A physical sign of a disease.

systemic infection An infection that invades the blood and spreads to other parts of the body.

toxin A poison.

vaccine A medicine that prevents disease by causing the body to build up immunity.

venereal disease A disease transmitted during sexual contact.

vibrios Curved forms of bacteria.

virus A particle made up of nucleic acid covered with a protein shell.

Further Reading

Arehart-Treihel, Joan. *Immunity: How Our Bodies Resist Disease.* New York: Holiday House, 1976.

Check, William A. *Encyclopedia of Health: AIDS.* New York: Chelsea House, 1988.

Kurland, Morton L. *Coping with AIDS: Facts and Fears.* New York: The Rosen Publishing Group, 1988.

Metos, Thomas H. *Communicable Diseases.* New York: Franklin Watts, 1987.

Patent, Dorothy Hinshaw. *Bacteria: How They Affect Other Living Things.* New York: Holiday House, 1980.

Patent, Dorothy Hinshaw. *Germs.* New York: Holiday House, 1983.

Taylor, Barbara. *Everything You Need to Know About AIDS.* New York: The Rosen Publishing Group, 1991 (revised).

Tully, Marianne. *Dread Diseases.* New York: Franklin Watts, 1978.

Wood, Samuel G. *Everything You Need to Know About Sexually Transmitted Diseases.* New York: The Rosen Publishing Group, 1990.

Index

Photo Credits:
P. 4: ©Blair Seitz/Photo Researchers, Inc.; p. 8: Biophoto Associates/Photo Researchers, Inc.; p. 10: ©Chris Bjornberg/Photo Researchers, Inc.; p. 16: CNRI/Science Photo Library/Photo Researchers, Inc.; p. 24: ©Larry Mulvehill/Photo Researchers, Inc.; p. 27: ©Mary Evans Picture Library/Photo Researchers, Inc.; p. 28: CDC/Science Source/Photo Researchers, Inc.; p. 32: ©Lowell Georgia/Science Source/Photo Researchers, Inc.; p. 33: March of Dimes/Photo Researchers, Inc.; p. 35: ©Pat and Tom Leeson/ Photo Researchers, Inc.; p. 37: Blackbirch Graphics, Inc.; p. 38: ©John Watney/Science/Photo Researchers, Inc.; p. 39: ©Mary Evans Picture Library/Photo Researchers, Inc.; p. 40: CNRI/Science Photo Library/Photo Researchers, Inc.; p. 45: CNRI/Science Photo Library/Photo Researchers, Inc.; p. 49: ©Dr. Jeremy Burgess/Science Photo Library/Photo Researchers, Inc.; p. 51: ©Alan D. Carey/Photo Researchers, Inc.; p. 56: ©Hank Morgan/Science Source/Photo Researchers, Inc.; p. 60: Will and Deni McIntyre/ Science Source/Photo Researchers, Inc.
Art and charts by Blackbirch Graphics.